MW01641628

Also by Shayla Raquel

Pre-Publishing Checklist

"The Rotting" (in the anthology *Shivers in the Night*)

The Suicide Tree

The 10 Commandments of Author Branding

All the Things I Should've Told You

poems on
love, grief & resilience

shayla raquel

All the Things I Should've Told You
First edition, February 2021

Curiouser Editing LLC
Yukon, OK
shaylaraquel.com

Editing: Sarah Liu, threefatesediting.com
Publishing and Design Services: Melinda Martin, melindamartin.me

ISBN: 978-1-7341357-3-2 (paperback)
978-1-7341357-4-9 (hardcover)

To Lauren Brooke Elena Alejandra De La Rosa-Hull:

I cannot wait to hug you in heaven.
I love you with all my heart.

Contents

A Letter from the Author

Poetry is an intimate moment between the writer and her soul.

And so, my most intimate moments from the last two years flood these pages. I let my soul bleed so I could heal.

Throughout my life, I have had scores of moments when I just wanted to say what was *truly* on my heart, but I didn't. So when I couldn't voice my feelings, I wrote them down. I was honest with myself when I couldn't be honest with others.

These are my innermost thoughts about love, grief, heartache, anger, and resiliency.

My hope is that at least one poem touches your soul and speaks to your heart.

Toxicity

No fangs sink in
No plant ingested
Nothing inhaled
Toxicity

My heart has blackened
My breathing is shallow
My pulse uneven
Toxicity

In my mind
In my soul
An oozing poison
Toxicity

I fell into the trap
A dumb prey
A perfect prey
Toxicity

You seep into my heart
You infect my core
You consume my world
Toxicity

The Past Tense

She was . . .
She was . . .
She was . . .

Why does he keep saying that about you?
The past tense version.
What's so bad about "is"?
That's how I still talk about you.

She was a leader.
She was a teacher.
She was a true legacy.

But now it's catching on. Oh, God, it's catching on.
They're all saying "She was . . ." now.
They've embraced the past tense,
and I can't even embrace a future without you.

She was . . .
She was . . .
She was . . .

Was is a dagger
that pierces my heart.

Was is an ending
that I don't want to read.

Was is a lie
that seeks to hurt.

And I know there will come a moment
when I say it too.
It'll slip out from my lips,
and I, unable to catch it in time,
will collapse in sorrow.

But for now, I'll remember you in the present.
I'll remember you the way you are.

She is . . .
She is . . .
She is . . .

In Heaven

When I meet you in heaven,
what would you like to do first?
Should we chat with Paul
who penned your life verse?

I could introduce you to my brother
or my nephew named Camdyn.
We could sing praises on high
and meet the Three Wise Men.

Will you show me your mansion
on your own hilltop, your door
open to all, and the glitter
that covers each inch of your floor?

Let's feast with Jesus and the twelve.
I'll order your favorite meal.
Our stomachs and hearts full,
we praise our Savior as we kneel.

We'll walk those golden streets,
as transparent as glass.
You count the dazzling gems
while divine angels pass.

At the end of a blissful day,
no tears will ever meet my eyes.
My heart will never feel pain again.
In heaven, there are no goodbyes.

Laceration

Bullets rain down,
piercing my skin,
each one sharper than the last—
an army of metal men.

I swerve and duck,
but you slice my heart,
your dagger hot with flames,
your skills a black art.

When my wounds heal,
the memories so raw,
will I fight once more?
Will I love despite your flaw?

Each cut, hole, and scar
led me to a deep confession:
You maimed me with words
and not a single weapon.

I Wish You Could See Your Potential

I wish you could see your potential—
your compassion that swells from
a bleeding heart, so quick to
help with nothing to gain.

I wish you would try, just try a little
to make something of yourself,
to embrace ambition the way you
grasp that stupid video game controller.

I wish you could see what I see.
Would things be different in your life
if you would've risen from the couch,
labored and toiled, and never languished?

I wish you would care, even for a minute,
about your future, your calling,
the three-day scruff, and those
tumultuous moments of silence.

But you wish for nothing,
because you're stagnant, contentment
wrapping its grip around your soul.
Around your potential.

Around what could've been.

The Day of Your Funeral

Hair, eyes, and lashes
Chestnut brown
Deep purple with glitter
Was Monday's gown

Hands overlapped
Nails polished and trim
Roses surround her
As eyes in tears swim

Puddles and whimpers
Framed photos, a dim light
She now walks gold streets
Jasper, emerald, sparkling white

No more pulse
But all around, her heart beats
A symbol of generosity
No human can defeat

All love, all zest
Her legacy as big as her smile
We'll say so long for now
And embrace in a while

The Box

The box sits in my garage,
as it has for a year.
There's nothing special about it.
But at one time,
its contents were meaningful.

A black-and-white scarf
(those thin tassels at the end).
I never liked scarves
until you wrapped one around me
on a blustery December day.

An oversized picture frame.
You + Me with a heart
where our smiling faces once lived.
The photo? That day in your driveway.
You remember, don't you?
The sun too bright in our eyes.
But we smiled anyway,
because we couldn't help it.

A leather Fossil purse.
Not from you. From your mom.
She really liked me, and I really liked her.
The purse went unused.
Much like her phone number is now.

One day I'll give the box to charity
so someone else can find joy in
our nearly new memories,
our tattered, inside-joke memories.

For now,
the box remains in my garage,
staring at me each time I pull my car inside.
When will I ever drop off that stupid box?
When will I let go?
I thought I had.

But I remember the Christmas when we
each said something we were thankful for,
a memory we cherished too.
I remember when I sang to you,
and your whole family laughed and sang along.
Mariah Carey, wasn't it?

But I remember
when you played the piano in the afternoon,
a melody I still hum.

I'm sorry it didn't work out.
I'm sorry I put you through it all.
I'm sorry I wasn't who you deserved.
I'm sorry to give away the last of our memories.
But I can't look at them anymore.

And by the way,
what did you do with your memories of me?
Do they collect dust in a garage too?

Or did you burn them all in a rush when she took my place?
Does my book live under your bed?
Or did it go in the trash?

Wherever my memories are,
Whatever you did with them,
I'm glad we had them.
I'm sorry we didn't have more.

Love at First Taste

I'm sorry I fell in love with you.
It wasn't planned.
I tried to stay away,
but you drew me in.

You stole more than my heart—
a thief in the night.
You lured me out of safety—
love at first sight.

I tried to give you up
time and time again.
I kicked you out, said my goodbyes,
but you moved back in.

No need to sweep me off my feet;
I was already on cloud nine.
Yet things took a harsh turn—
I stepped way out of line.

So I fought back, fists clenched,
the romance now crumbled.
I can offer my love elsewhere.
I pray I won't stumble.

No Thank You

I dreamed I was to be seated for dinner
with men and women from God's Word.
"Jesus Christ, the savior of each sinner,
will arrive at the table," I overheard.

But I could not sit next to the Samaritan girl.
She had been married five times!
With a quick, dignified whirl,
I distanced myself from her crimes.

"No thank you," I said.

An offer to sit with a man came my way.
Wretched sores covered every limb.
"A leper!" I exclaimed. I couldn't stay.
For me, the sight was just too grim.

"No thank you," I said.

Another man waved, wearing fancy clothes.
A short man, he collected tax.
So I turned up my nose.
Who could forgive that greedy act?

"No thank you," I said.

A third man, so handsome and strong,
gave me a kind smile, but my eyes widened then.
An adulterer, a murderer—how wrong!
I would *not* sit at the table with him.

"No thank you," I said.

Perhaps this woman would suit.
The first-ever female—it was Eve.
I knew then she had eaten that serpent's fruit.
How could she have been so naive?

"No thank you," I said.

This continued on down the line.
Drunks, liars, murderers, cheats.
They were all there to dine.
By the end of the table, I had no seat.

I stood alone as my dream came to an end.
The door opened, and a light shone so bright.
A man with holes in his wrists entered in.
My savior was an unforgettable sight.

The man who died on that mount
did not sit at his own lavish meal.
He greeted all his guests—no matter the count.
My embarrassment I could not conceal.

He talked to the first evangelist.
He thanked the mighty king of Israel.
He ate with little Zacchaeus.
And he hugged the man whose sores were visible.

My savior did not pick and choose.
He loved each person the same.
And not once did he accuse—
not once did he bring shame.

I awoke with a start.
What had I become?
From this Pharisaic body I will depart.
I had never felt so numb.

Where was my compassion?
What about God's never-ending mercy?
My tear-streaked face was now ashen.
Of his love I am forever unworthy.

Suddenly Jesus Christ was in my room.
He said: "I love you no matter what you've done."
The man who rose from that dark tomb
willingly forgave me—and everyone.

Then my savior approached my side.
He earnestly asked, "May I sit here too?"
And so I sincerely cried:
"Yes, thank you."

Bitterness

I sacrificed everything for you.
Turbulent planes, credit card surprises.
A piece of my heart.
A chunk of my soul.

I believed you were worth fighting for.
Feuding with those I love.
Shouting matches, ignored "I love yous."
And for what?

Suddenly all I resolved to renounce
met with all you forced me to yield.
Instantly inseparable,
together they ignited a new emotion.

Bitterness.
A growing, burning poison.
A monster in my heart.
Bound to torment me.

I subdued the bitterness,
if only for a moment.
But it awakens at inopportune times,
slithering past me with a mind of its own.

So I cry for you,
because I miss you,
because I love you,
because I hate you.

I let you go so the fighting would stop.
And it did. Everyone got what they wanted.
While they relished in their win,
you ravished her.

Now I'm ten months out,
and for the life of me,
I can't conquer this bitterness,
though God knows I've tried.

How do I burn the bitterness
that freezes my very core?
How do I forgive you
when I can't forgive myself?

Heartbreak

I'm no stranger to heartbreak.
Old friends, we go way back.
Years of memories.
More still to come.

My erstwhile friend shows up
when I should've seen him a mile away.
Always sneaking up on me.
Two steps ahead.

When he comes to say hello,
he holds me too close, too tight.
I ask for space.
He overstays his welcome.

I Lied

I told you a lot of things.
Some of them were true.
Some were not.

I told you I wanted a break.
I told you to slow down.
I told you I need time to think.

I lied I lied I lied

I told you we were cool.
I told you we're just friends.
I told you she's better for you.

I lied I lied I lied

Killin' Me

I can't read your mind, baby.
Tell me what you're thinkin'.
Whisper it in my ear.
Be straight with me.

But you hem and haw.
You beat around the bush.
You smirk and shrug.

And it's killin' me,
killin' me,
killin' me
in the dead of the night.

Just tell me how you feel, baby.
I'll listen, I swear.
I'll drink in your words.
I'll soak them up.

But you grow silent.
You don't talk.
You ignore the question mark.

And it's killin' me,
killin' me,
killin' me
when I look in those green eyes.

Spit it out.
Stop holding back.
Let it all flow freely.
I'm ready to know the truth.

But you hold back.
You restrain.
You let the nerves get the best of you.

And, honey, I don't know if you want me
or not.
But I guess you could say,
it's killin' me not to tell you
that I need you.

Stagnant

The river used to flow, didn't it?
A vague recollection in my mind.
It once gushed with fervor.
Filling the riverbed so high.
    Stagnant.

Did the river dry up overnight,
or did it drain over the years?
Cascades that fed into waterfalls
now drip like a water faucet.
    Stagnant.

Or is there not a drop felt?
Is the river now as desolate as the Sahara?
How long must I quench?
When will I no longer thirst?
    Stagnant.

I do not float in the river anymore.
There is no water to take me.
I'm part of the cracked earth now.
Unable to move, dried up.
    Stagnant.

Family

You are blood,
But you aren't family.
You look like me,
But you're my enemy.
You share my surname,
But you rob me of my sanity.
You are of my lineage,
But you created a tragedy.

Cruelty

How could you be this cruel?
Or do you think you're innocent?

Innocent as you stab me in the back.
Innocent as you call me reprehensible.
Innocent as you ransack my home.

How could you be this cruel?
Or do you think it's warranted?

Warranted to lie about me.
Warranted to read my diary.
Warranted to whisper it all.

How could you be this cruel?
Or do you think it's necessary?

Necessary to kick me while I'm down.
Necessary to ostracize me.
Necessary to take, take, take.

But I will rise.
I will wipe my back clean of blood.
I will put my home back together.
I will silence the whispers.
I will fix what you have broken.

Because I am not cruel.

Freedom

You are the clanking dishes in a busy restaurant.
You are the embrace of an old friend.
You are the sweet scent of a candle at a farmers market.
You are the first sip of a frothy latte at my favorite café.

Why did I take you for granted?
No one told me you could disappear.
Aren't you permanent?
Constant.
Infinite.
Eternal.

Now, the unspeakable thing,
that illness whose name we hate to utter,
devours more than its victims—
it consumes you too.

Mouth open.
Claws out.
Pure darkness in its belly.

Why did I take you for granted?
I can't see you anymore, but I can feel
your waning presence.
Won't you come back?
Return.
Fight.
Stay.

But this leviathan is swallowing you whole,
gulping you down like weak prey.
And what have I done to rescue you?
Fight for you.
Stand up for you.
Cling to you.

Why did I take you for granted?
I miss what we once had.
Come mend my broken heart.
Repair.
Restore.
Revive.

I'm sorry I took you for granted.
I thought we had all the time in the world.
I was wrong; we were all wrong.
We'll make it up to you.

The Same Way

You told me you loved me today,
and yet, I couldn't tell you
I loved you the same way.

I want to love you—
be yours forever and always.
Truly, truly I do.

I'll tell you instead, if it's all right,
that I think of you each day
and I long for you every night.

I miss you even when you're with me
and I yearn for your touch.
When I close my eyes, you're all I see.

One day, baby, one day,
I'll hold you close and tell you,
I love you the same way.

Email

"Checking on you."
I didn't need to see the sender to know
who it was.

It's you. It's always you.

You wanted to make sure I was okay
with everything going on.
I had been thinking of you too.

So I told you how I was, kept it cool.
But, oh God, I left out so much.
I didn't tell you it all.

It's you. It's always you.

I held back. I held it all in.
I didn't tell you about those sleepless nights
when I ached for one more embrace.

I didn't tell you how much it hurt to say goodbye.
I didn't tell you that I still love you.
I didn't tell you that I wish I was her.

It's you. It's always you.

You told me about work.
You told me about the family.
You told me about the dog.

But you didn't tell me you dreamed of me.
You do still, don't you?
I know I dream of you.

It's you. It's always you.

You tiptoed around the obvious.
"I missed you."
Oh, I more than miss you.

I long for you. I desire just one more minute with you.
One more minute for me to wrap
my arms around your legs
and beg for forgiveness.

It's you. It's always you.

Yet you already forgave me.
Why? Why did you do something I don't deserve?
Because that's the type of person you are.

I know we need to stop.
This conversation must end.
You've checked on me now.

It's you. It's always you.

But we can't stop, can we?
We fell back into our old ways.
It was so easy.

I've missed this.
I've missed us.
You've missed me too, haven't you?

It's me. It's always me.

To the People Who Broke My Heart

I'm sorry.

I'm sorry I cried on the sofa at midnight.
At the booth in my favorite restaurant.
In the parked car on a bright day.
In the arms of loved ones.
In my bed alone.

I'm sorry I shed tears for you.
And you too.
For the things you have said.
For the things you have done.

I'm sorry I let your words slice my skin.
(*Reprehensible*)
Cutting deeper at every syllable.
(*Unrepentant*)
Until the blood flowed like a stream.
(*Unremorseful*)

I'm sorry you're miserable
and take it out on me.
I'm sorry you're vengeful
and kick me when I'm down.

I'm sorry you lied,
because you're better when you don't.
I'm sorry you hurt me,
because I remember when you didn't.

I'm sorry you think I'm someone I'm not.
I'm sorry you tarnish my name.
I'm sorry you have nothing better to do.

Oh, but most of all,
I'm so terribly sorry I believed you.

I'm sorry I believed your words had merit.
Had value.
Had weight.
That they mattered.

I'm so sorry I let you hurt me.
I'm so sorry you were cruel.
I'm so sorry you're not sorry.

But I'm not sorry for getting back up.
For bleeding out your poison.
For standing a little taller when I felt small.

I'm not sorry for hugging you
(your tears stained my dress,
the one you called skanky)
while you admitted what I already knew.

I'm not sorry for telling you,
"It's going to be okay, I love you,
I won't judge you, I'm here."

I'm not sorry for driving you home,
getting you into bed,
giving you snacks,
and just sitting with you in that moment.

I'm not sorry I did what you could never do:
love unfailingly.
Just love someone no matter what they have done.
Just love someone who is hurting.
Just love someone who did wrong.
Just love someone who is struggling.
Just love someone who needs comfort.

I'm sorry you couldn't do that.
I'm sorry you couldn't love me when I needed you the most.
I'm sorry you crucified me when I needed to heal.

I'm sorry, so very sorry, that you broke my heart.
Because you were a part of my heart too.

Impatient

Impatient, impatient, impatient.
You're in too much of a hurry.
I was thirty-five.
Just wait.

What do you think I've been doing?
I wait in my bed alone each night.
I amble to parties without a date.
I attend as a maid of honor, no veil.

Impatient, impatient, impatient.
It'll happen when it happens.
You always move too fast.
Why can't you just sit tight?

Oh, but I sit alone at night.
And I wish for a husband to kiss me.
I wish for a chance at love.
Isn't thirty years enough?

When We Planned Your Funeral

The mini fridge hums behind me.
We sit at a long wooden table with cushy chairs.
The director boots up his laptop.
Your mom takes deep breaths, steadying herself.

"How many copies of the death certificate will you need?"

Candles whose wicks have never been lit rest on the table.
The lighting is dim in here.
A loose sweatshirt hangs off your mom's frail body.
Her hair is long, like yours, and lies on her shoulders.

"Can you spell that name for me?"

The director types with precision.
He wears gold-rimmed glasses, his sideburns too long.
Your dad's chin rests in his closed fist.
He breaks down first at "open casket."

"I want her to look good before you have a visitation date for a full viewing."

Your mascara has to be big.
Your hair has to be bigger.
You wouldn't want it any other way.
Your mom asks about a date.

"I'm still working on her and would strongly suggest you wait."

We can't have the funeral this weekend.
It'll have to wait till Monday.
Whimpers leave your dad, he looks down.
What about the viewing?

"It's going to take me a couple of full days."

It still didn't click what he meant.
Tactfully, finally, he explained about the broken glass
from the car wreck.
It goes everywhere; your arm needs more work.

"Do you have a cardigan or sweater to help?"

But your mom didn't even think about your arm,
so she sobs into her hands.
Tissues are nearby, someone reaches.
Your dad tries to comfort her.

"The last thing you want is to rush something like this."

All the Things I Should've Told You

My sorrow starts as a steady stream
until the tears run like rapids,
spilling . . .
bursting . . .
gushing . . .

And I can't dam the grief
because, you see, there are things I should've told you.

I should've told you about your eyes
and the way they fluttered.
Deep pools of chocolate.

I should've told you about your big heart
and how charitable you were:
replacing worn shoes,
paying for her night school,
handing me that locket.

I should've told you about your smile
and how it lit up the whole room.
A contagious smile.
A radiant smile.
A forget-about-the-bad-in-the-world smile.

I should've told you about the boy who loved you,
about the look in his adoring eyes.

I should've told you to stay the night again.
To braid my hair one more time.
To snuggle in my bed again.
To fall asleep on my couch one more time.

Oh, I should've told you so many things,
but I never did.
So I'm telling you now.

I'm telling you all the things I should've told you before.
You had a real laugh.
A hearty laugh.
A don't-hold-back laugh.
A let-it-fly laugh.

Your hair cascaded down your shoulders,
the waves voluminous,
billowing.
Rippling.
A current.

You taught us to do better:
to strive for greatness,
to embrace our dreams,
to do something that matters.

You were spunky
yet poised.
You were zealous
yet gracious.

You had a legacy,
one of heart, style, and smile,
and an unforgettable hunger
to change lives.

That's exactly what you did:
you changed our lives.
You stole our hearts.
You taught us unabating love.

So I won't dam my tears just yet,
and maybe I never will,
because, sweet girl,
I still have so much more to tell you.

Mosaic

You saw the shards
of my broken heart
and gingerly picked them up.

You gathered them all
in your steady, capable hands
even as the glass sliced your skin.

You pieced them together
until an image formed,
and you reached for the glue.

You sealed your creation
and brought it to me,
a gift unlike any other.

You mended my heart
and created a mosaic
of love.

OCEAN

Only in the emerald waves
Can I be wild and untamed,
Exhilarated as the water engulfs me
And sweeps me into the deep,
Never demanding anything at all.

I Love You

It was two weeks, six days in.
You were going to say it the night before,
but you didn't, and I didn't,
because we thought we were crazy for
    saying *those three words.*

It was two weeks, six days in.
And you said it first.
My lips latched onto yours,
and I replied the same,
    saying *those three words.*

It was two weeks, six days in.
And we said it over and over,
drowning ourselves in that first moment,
growing hoarse in lamplight,
    saying *those three words.*

The Race to You

Every bad breakup
Every sleepless night
Every set of puffy eyes

Every man who ghosted
Every unanswered text
Every single lie

Every third wheel
Every angry prayer
Every blocked number

Every moment of heartache
I'd do it all over again
Because it was worth it
To get to you

Just Some Memories

Remember that night on my white pleather couch?
Your hands were a pillow as you leaned on the armrest.
We tried to tell you to go to bed,
but you fought slumber the way you fought negativity
    with all your might.

Remember when we sat high in the skyscraper?
You ordered the same as me: steak.
Why were you so quiet that night?
Did he make you nervous? Did you love him
    with all your heart?

Remember when I babysat you?
You and your sisters painted my face.
At that age, you were so dedicated.
I knew you'd strive for greatness
    with all your soul.

Remember when you cut my old sock
and used it to perform magic with my hair?
A messy bun, but there was nothing messy about it.
I should've paid better attention to your skill,
    but I didn't.

I thought you'd always be there to do it for me.

Wrapped Up

I don't hear the people cheering
as we kiss in the dimly lit parking lot.
I don't feel the wind lift up my hair
and gently sweep it into your face.

I'm just wrapped up in you.

I don't listen to the voice in my head
telling me to slow down—it's too fast.
I don't notice the hands on the clock
as they stop time only for us.

I'm just wrapped up in you.

I don't sense the world stopping
as we succumb to pure bliss.
I don't see the sky burst into flames
while my lips search for yours.

I'm just wrapped up in you.

In the Moment

The sun set, but you missed it.
It was every shade of pink on the lake.
As it took a dip in the water,
my lips were on your cheek.
And so you said:

"I'm just in the moment."

The passersby strolled along, but you didn't notice.
My flowery dress blew in the wind,
and the scent of your cologne followed it.
I breathed you in.
And so you said:

"I'm just in the moment."

Water hit the rocks, but you didn't hear them crash.
You listened instead to my fervent whispers.
Then my laugh, boisterous and genuine,
floated to your ears.
And so you said:

"I'm just in the moment."

It turned dark, but you never saw the blackened heavens.
The lighthouse shone blue and red in late summer.
Nighttime swept over us.
There was no moon, but there were stars in your eyes.
And so you said:

"I'm just in the moment."

The world ended, but you didn't flinch.
Your eyes connected with mine,
and they wouldn't have left if the earth imploded.
You held your gaze, and I tried to stay steady.
And so I asked,

"Are you just in the moment?"

Pining

I can love you from afar,
can't I?
I don't have to tell a soul,
do I?

Do you even notice me
when I walk by?
Or do you see right through me,
an invisible cloak over my skin?

It's juvenile, I know,
but I pine for you
in the dead of the day,
desiring your touch.

I think about our kiss.
Not the first, no;
the most recent one.
Your taste on my lips.

Do you think of that too?
Or was it a regret?
You never talk about it.
But I guess I don't know either.

Hang On to Me

Kiss me in the park
on that bench with the friendly ducks.
Kiss me when it's 100 degrees out,
my hair sticking to my forehead.

I think I'll hang on to you.

Push me on the swing
and let my toes reach the sky.
Tell me funny stories
and act them out in the crowded coffee shop.

I think I'll hang on to you.

Tell me about my blue eyes;
stare deep, get lost a little.
Tuck my hair behind my ear
and drag your lips across mine.

I think I'll hang on to you.

Buy me dinner on a Saturday night
and share your dessert with me.
Beg me not to leave.
Whisper again and again, "Five more minutes."

I think I'll hang on to you.

Pinky promise me something,
but don't let go of my hand.
Interlock your fingers with mine
and turn up the music.

I think I'll hang on to you.

Push my buttons, annoy me.
Throw your head back and laugh.
Embarrass me, make me blush.
Waggle your eyebrows, rub your nose to mine.

I think I'll hang on to you.

Become breathless with me
on a night like this
when those clouds turn as pink as my cheeks
and you hold me with those capable arms.

I think I'll hang on to you.

Fire

A knock on the door
My breath catches
I'm expecting you
A turn of the knob
  Flicker

No words needed
You scratch your nape
A forced chuckle
I murmur a hello
  Spark

You take a seat
Forearms on your knees
My gaze meets your blues
A dimple, a leer
  Glow

I sit with you
And you lean in
Your lips tremble
Then they meet mine
  Ignite

And everything stops
Only to be set ablaze

  Burning
    Scorching
      Smoldering

The kiss is over
The world is moving now
Our thoughts entwined
Our moment done
    Extinguish

Good Night

I couldn't sleep tonight,
so I thought of you
and wished it'd all turn out right.

I sat up in bed,
memories fading here and there;
but one stuck in my head
that I couldn't bear
      to lose.

Maybe you're dreaming now—
a million miles away—
of what I'm thinking now,
dreaming of what to say
      to me.

I saw it in your eyes,
and you saw it in mine.
In your perfect heart, therein lies
a love, so pure and fine,
      for me.

You couldn't sleep tonight
because you thought of me
and how it's all turning out right.

Only You

With every whisper
and with every touch,
I fall a little harder,
harder than before.

I try to pretend
like it's not happening to me,
but I can't hide it anymore.
And, baby, neither can you.

With each kiss
and with each embrace,
My heart flutters, it soars.
But then . . .

I try to pretend
like this isn't real,
and you're just a figment,
only to vanish in the end.

But with those eyes
and with those lips,
this just can't be real.
But then all I feel is . . .

Your love.
Your love is all I need.
All I need to know is that you're here
and that you'll be mine.

I tried to pretend
like I wasn't falling for you,
and it wasn't until I fell so hard
that I knew
it was you
and only you.

Are You Awake?

I wonder if he's awake.
Is he thinking of me,
or am I lost in my thoughts
once again?

He looked so regal.
And I whispered,
"I'm so in love with you,"
but he couldn't hear me.

I wonder if he's awake.
Is he lost in thought
in another world
thinking of me?

His smile caught me,
dragged me to another place.
And I forgot my name,
but I'm used to that with him.

I go back to our kiss,
and it's so consuming,
But does he remember?
Or is it old news?

Others vie for my affection,
but I wave them off
as I steal another moment with him—
just a brief kiss.

I watch him and fall in love harder.
I keep it to myself,
hoping he'll notice,
but then what?

What will we do then?
Run away? Start a life together?
I think not.
For now, I'll remain in the shadows.

Just a Crush

I am so in love with you.
And I am so sorry,
because I didn't mean to fall so hard.
I thought I had it under control.
    Just a crush.

But you swept me off my feet,
and I latched on.
Hook. Line. And sinker.
And I can't concentrate.
    Just a crush.

The thing is,
I don't think that was ever your plan:
to claim my heart like you did.
Is it accidental love?
    Just a crush.

In My Eyes

Gold specks around the sky blue of your eyes.
Fingers through your sandy brown hair.
Rugged hands on my delicate ones.

Brawny arms, muscular shoulders.
Supple lips, brilliant smile.
Rosy cheeks, ruddy skin.
Thick beard, kissable nose.

Hearty laughter fills the room.
Silly faces, goofy dances.
Clever jokes, romantic gestures.
Sweet whispers, thousands of "I love yous."

To Me

Stay in your treehouse longer.
Make another blanket fort.
Take more risks.
Ignore the bullies.
Wipe your tears.
Visit her in the hospital.
Believe in yourself for once.
Close your eyes at the funeral.
Go to that family reunion at the lake.
Hug her for a little while longer.
Leave those toxic people.
Say no again and again.
Say yes more and more.
Play hide-and-seek with your niece.
Just let him go already.
Stop fighting with them.
Have faith in your abilities.
Take more time off.
Log off.
Take back what you said.
Pay attention to what He's saying.
Block out jealousy.
Hike with your dad.
Stand up for what you believe in.
Embrace your talents.
Walk deeper into the ocean.
Vote your conscience.
Build your empire.

Kiss your soul mate.
Snuggle your nephews.
Throw away those mementos.
Slap him right in the face.
Laugh right in her face.
Save every penny.
Recognize deceit.
Watch your mom as she cooks.
Appreciate more sunrises.
Visit your grandpa in Clinton.
Find out for yourself.
Take nothing for granted.

So *This* Is Love

This is love?
After all these years,
the love I have for you
is unlike anything I've ever known.

This is love?
All this time
I thought I knew
what love was.

This is love?
The void in my heart
finally filled,
I'm complete.

This is love?
I never knew
it felt like this.
It's different.

This is love?
Look at what I've been missing.
How have I survived
without this love?

Love Is

Love is
When you hold my hand
As I tiptoe on the ice-covered sidewalk.

Love is
When you roll up your sleeves
And scrub my forgotten dishes.

Love is
When you hug me tight
As tears flow down my cheeks.

Love is
When you surprise me
With my favorite chocolate on a lonely day.

Love is
When you write me a note
On that little pink Post-It.

Love is
When you slow dance with me
On my back porch to no music.

Love is
When you tilt my chin up
And kiss me on the lips.

Love is
You.

When Was It?

Did you fall in love with me on the bench?
The one that faced the lake
as the lighthouse curiously towered over us.

Did you fall in love with me in the parking lot?
When we danced in the late summer breeze,
all alone except for the faint music.

Did you fall in love with me at my front door?
The one that hung open for ten minutes
after we said good night a dozen times.

Did you fall in love with me in the quiet morning?
When you opened your eyes and thought of me
laughing as you swung me around the room.

Did you fall in love with me at the end of this poem?
The one I wrote in the middle of the night
when I fell in love with you.

An expert editor, best-selling author, and book marketer, Shayla Raquel works one-on-one with writers every day. A lifelong lover of books, she has been in the publishing industry for ten years and specializes in self-publishing.

Her award-winning blog teaches new and established authors how to write, publish, and market their books.

She is the author of the *Pre-Publishing Checklist*, "The Rotting" (in *Shivers in the Night*), *The Suicide Tree, The 10 Commandments of Author Branding*, and *All the Things I Should've Told You*. In her not-so-free time, she acts as organizer for the Yukon Writers' Society, studies all things true crime, and obsesses over squirrels. She lives in Oklahoma with her dogs, Chanel, Wednesday, and Baker.

Connect with the Author

shaylaraquel.com

Leave a Review

If you enjoyed *All the Things I Should've Told You*,
will you consider leaving a review
on your platform of choice?